PANACEA
HEALING WORDS

DIYA TRIVEDI

Copyright © Diya Trivedi
All Rights Reserved.

ISBN 978-1-68509-358-7

This book has been published with all efforts taken to make the material error-free after the consent of the author. However, the author and the publisher do not assume and hereby disclaim any liability to any party for any loss, damage, or disruption caused by errors or omissions, whether such errors or omissions result from negligence, accident, or any other cause.

While every effort has been made to avoid any mistake or omission, this publication is being sold on the condition and understanding that neither the author nor the publishers or printers would be liable in any manner to any person by reason of any mistake or omission in this publication or for any action taken or omitted to be taken or advice rendered or accepted on the basis of this work. For any defect in printing or binding the publishers will be liable only to replace the defective copy by another copy of this work then available.

DEDICATING TO MY LOVED ONES

AND TO ONE'S WHO HELPED ME THROUGHOUT

Contents

Foreword vii

Preface ix

SHE-FAA

1. Saturation 3
2. Self Love 5
3. She 7
4. Still Awake 9
5. Self Empowerment 11
6. Sky By The Sea 13
7. Seprate Hearts 15
8. Sprinting Time 17
9. Solitariness 19
10. Synchronal Happiness 21
11. Sentience 23

REVAMPING

12. Mental Illness 27
13. Chasing Perfection 29
14. You Are Powerful 31
15. Theft Of Joy 33
16. Be Kind 35
17. Small Things 37
18. Hold On 39
19. Do Something New 41
20. You Are Enough 43

Foreword

i) With a heart brimming with emotions the poet Diya Trivedi spills them in letters and words forming these sublime poetic pieces. The emotions dealt with are not extraordinary; they are familiar and relatable , reflecting on the agony one feels at different phases of life.

The diverse thoughts behind the poems stem from the identity crisis fostered by insecurities,inferiority complex and lack of affection that people encounter, especially in this mordern time. Whether it is the quest for self-love, validation and hapiness or the torment of unrequited love, Trivedi delves deep into the issues. Referring to the readers in second person, the poet engages in a lyrical conversation with the readers, hoping to be a companion to the aching hearts. However, a few of them are written in the first person that open a window for the readers to know their poet and be a confidante to her confessions wherein she lays bare her inner psyche.

These twenty poems, in short are about to take you through a ride admist the tumultuous emotions one experiences in the course of the journey called life

   - Tanisha

   @books.reviews.and.more.

   ii) Panacea by Diya Trivedi is a delightful read, a book full of varied emotions written by the poetess, meticulously. The beauty of her poems lies in the fact that poems are written straight from her heart and reaches the heart of the reader with quite ease. In her little melange of emotions she has written about self love, empowerment, love, kindness and nature beautifully. After reading her poems your heart is filled with positivity, peace and goodness. I thoroughly enjoyed reading Panacea and I am sure every reader will be touched by the simplicity and goodness of her poetry. I wish Diya Trivedi a great success in her endeavours.

- Monika kapur

@therealmonikakapur

iii) Poems from panacea by Diya Trivedi are really fascinating they are more than real most of poems lies in what we go through daily. Poetries are mixture of emotions that we really face when we start growing. I loved going through book panacea and I am sure every reader will love it too.

- Prem parekh

@es._.obligatorio

Preface

Born in 2003, Diya Trivedi had her early education in prestigious school in Ahmedabad, Gujarat.

A widely read person with on going graduation and a professional course.

She have accomplishment span the fields of sports, reading, writing and public speaking . Panacea is her second book she started writing poetries back in 2019 .

Finding purpose to every little things is what keeps her insane.

You can write to her at - diyatrivedi2312@gmail.com

PREFACE

SHE-FAA

1. SATURATION

You hide your pain
So that others don't feel it as their own
You cry while showering
And while you're driving alone
These are the moments when you can't escape your head
Filling you with a stomach- twisted dread
Memories saturated with regret and sorrow
You withstand today just to feel more severely tomorrow
You want to heal the deep fractures of your soul
But sometimes what is required takes too much of all
As it is you can barely breathe
Not really sure how to save me

2. SELF LOVE

Do you like what you see
When you lay your eyes on me
Is it wrong
That i constantly seek outside validation
That i won't believe that I'm pretty
Unless you say so
But how do I
How could I
Possibly
Love myself
If i keep relying on love from someone else ?

3. SHE

It hurts
Somewhere deep inside
Screams of agony
Sending waves of pain
From the core
Straight through
Striking the surface
Of my fragile skin
A terrified little girl
Trapped within her own thoughts
Whilst her mind plays the victim
But who would suspect
She was such a mess
With a smile to kill
And a heart full of kidness

4. STILL AWAKE

When it is late
When it is dark
I sit alone with my thoughts
Acknowledging the silence
Of the world
I physically inhabit
A certain peace
I crave for
Inside my own mind
Each thought gettinng
And clearer
With time

5. SELF EMPOWERMENT

I wish
for once
that I would not
beg god
to make me beautiful ,
loved,
appreciated
I know I don't have
the face,
the body ,
the people ,
the hapiness that I have something
good inside me
or just a feeling that I have something
Maybe all I have are
prayers I breath every night into my
pillows
and the ugly me
Whom no one would behold even
mistakenly
not even I
Would I never be what I want to be ?

6. SKY BY THE SEA

She looks to the sky
And she finds
Not him , not her
But all, and nothing
A nil search
For the one answer
The ultimate life enhancer
Neither a fullstop
Or a question

7. SEPRATE HEARTS

I look into your eyes
And there
I notice a familiar pain
Tears welling up inside
And it all feels like
Yesterday again
Such vivid memories
It has been such a long time
since i admired the rain
Two broken hearts
Love could drive anyone insane.

8. SPRINTING TIME

The more time that passes
The more angry I am at the
World for spinning -
Angry at the minutes , hours ,
Even seconds for passing me by-
For taking me further away from you -
Further away from your memory
Time has kidnapped you
And made me it's prisoner

9. SOLITARINESS

I've danced
In circles
Waiting
For the day
You would
Appear
And turn me
The right way
I've looked out
To the stars at night
Hoping your light
Would remove
Any fright
I feel
When removing
Monsters from
Under my bed
Or the demons
That play havoc
In my head
I often wonder
How many
Of them,
Are mine ?
Or if you

And grandad
Ran out of time
To take them
With you

10. SYNCHRONAL HAPPINESS

I have been the happiest when I am in control
And things are going the way I see fit
The minute change walks through the door ,
I lose my shit
Unaware that my emotions
Are controlled by my circumstances .
I try my best to cope with inconsistency ,
But I panic when things become too big for me .
Begging and pleading doesn't seem to faze God .
So , I've learned to pray for peace instead
Peace knowing someone greater is in control,
Peace knowing his way
May not always be a walk in the park.
Peace gives me the option to choose hapiness.
And hapiness is something I choose to be ,
Regardless of what is going on around me .
I have surrendered control ,
Now I am set free.

PANACEA

11. SENTIENCE

When you pulled the air
From my lungs,
Did you use it to sing
A beautiful song?
When you drained the blood
From my veins,
Did a brush stroke it
Like an oil paint?
When you claimed
Every inch of my skin,
Did you envision it as a canvas
Or a perfect print?
When you ripped from my chest
My beating heart,
Did you at least make my death
A work of art

REVAMPING

12. MENTAL ILLNESS

Sometimes I wonder why
I never spoke up at all
I preferred living in my head
Where I built a giant wall
It's miles high and miles long
No way around or through
I've created many escape plans
But escape , I never do
Instead the wall grows higher
Brick placed on top of brick
Now I fear there's no way out
Of a wall that's grown this thick

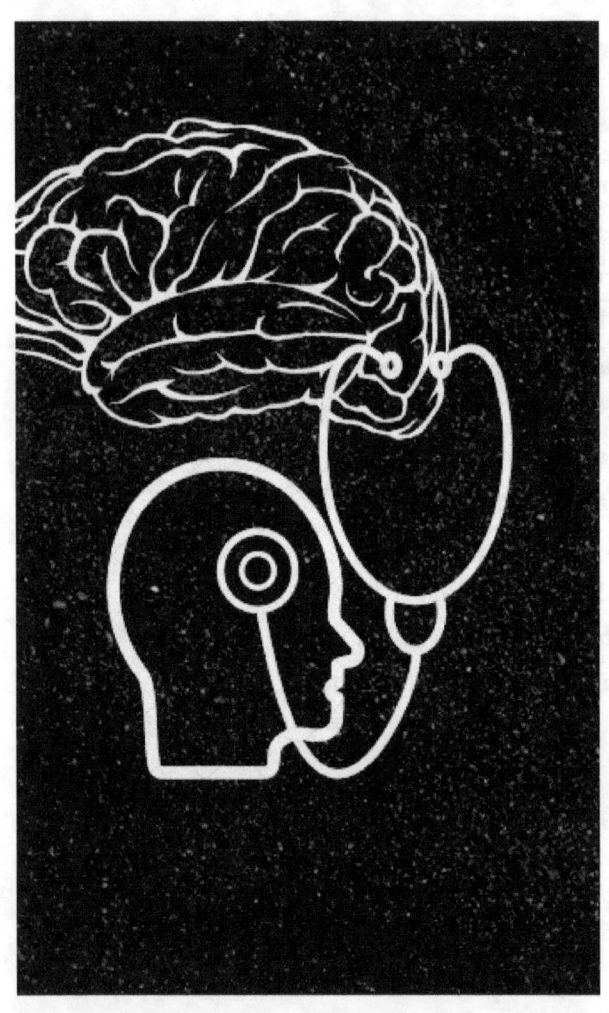

13. CHASING PERFECTION

Chasing perfection
Will have you aimlessly wandering
In all the wrong directions
Because there is no such thing
As being perfect
And chasing that fairytale
Will never be worth it
Find the beauty in the
So called 'imperfections'
That are the reason you turn away
From your own reflection
Dive deep into introspection
And only come up for air
When you've found the beauty within
Because being beautiful
Is not at all about the skin
You live in
I'd rather be beautiful
For my heart and my soul
Than to be nothing more
Than someone's "body goals"
So instead of wandering
In the wrong direction
Embrace the fact that there is

No such thing as perfection

14. YOU ARE POWERFUL

Today I dare you ,
I challenge you actually ,
To lift your eyes to that staircase of life ,
To place your feet , though uncertain
On the first step,
To push yourself off that platform of self
Doubt , and to rise
To climb each step with confidence ,
Determination and strength
To know that you are powerful,
You can rise and emerge at the summit ,
Holding your head high ,
And shouting your victory to the
listening winds .

15. THEFT OF JOY

The bitter taste of envy
Is the greatest theft of joy
Envy doen't main the target
It's you that she'll destroy
Pouring all your energy
Wishing failure on someone else
Will not gain you anything
But animosity within yourself
So stop envy in her tracks
Before she steals your peace
Replacing envy with self-love
Is the most worthwhile feat

16. BE KIND

Not everyone cracks the
same way,
Not everyone's scars are
Hidden or on display,
Not everyone heals and
Mends at the same rate.
So be patient, ever loving,
And always kind,
Try to always have your
Fellow neighbour in mind.

PANACEA

17. SMALL THINGS

Do you know what I find absolutely enthralling?
The fact that we put so much effort into "big"
Things, in things that would catch someone's eye
Or grip their heart,
Yet,
With what little effort we put
Into our genuine smiles,
Our loud and reverent laughs,
That is what draws people,
What makes their breath catch,
What stops them in their tracks,
So my love,
Stop putting so much effort into being noticed,
And start noticing the small beautiful things.

18. HOLD ON

I'm not sure what battle you're fighting
What demons you're facing,
How many tears you're shedding
But I do know this;
You will win,
You are strong and bold and beautiful,
Hold on my love,
Victory is brewing,
And it's just a breath away.

19. DO SOMETHING NEW

I know you would rather leave things
In a corner,
To try and forget,
To burn and bury and hide,
But doing so gathers dust and hate
And ash,
All of which can fill your lungs,
Suffocating you from the inside out.
So my love,
Its time to remove whatever it is you
placed in that corner,
And makes space for something new

20. YOU ARE ENOUGH

Gentle reminder,
Some days it is enough
To just exist,
Your presence alone is
Enough,
Don't feel pressured to
Be more, or do more,
Than you can offer
Today,
For you are enough,
Always and forever.

Dear readers I hope you enjoyed reading and I will see you in other book, Till then stay tuned!

Special thanks to -

Prem parekh

Dhruvi Dhagia

Viral Parmar

Tanisha

Monika kapur

And to one's who helped me through out

www.ingramcontent.com/pod-product-compliance
Lightning Source LLC
LaVergne TN
LVHW011859060526
838200LV00054B/4431